ADVENTURES
WITH ATOMS
AND MOLECULES

CHE FOR

ADVENTURES WITH ATOMS AND MOLECULES

BOOK I

CHEMISTRY EXPERIMENTS FOR YOUNG PEOPLE

ROBERT C. MEBANE

THOMAS R. RYBOLT

Enslow Publishers, Inc.

44 Fadem Road	PO Box 38
Box 699	Aldershot
Springfield, NJ 07081	Hants GU12 6BP
USA	UK

Library of Congress Cataloging-in-Publication Data

Mebane, Robert C.
 Adventures with atoms and molecules.
 Includes index.
 Summary: Chemistry experiments for home or school demonstrate the
properties and behavior of various kinds of atoms and molecules.
 1. Chemistry—Experiments—Juvenile literature. [1. Chemistry—Experiments.
2. Molecules—Experiments. 3. Experiments] I. Rybolt, Thomas R. II. Title.
QD38.M43 1985 540'.78 85-10177
ISBN 0-7660-1224-7 (pbk)

Printed in the United States of America

10 9 8 7 6 5 4 3 2 1

Cover Illustration: © Corel Corporation

ACKNOWLEDGEMENT

We wish to thank Alice Garvin, Ann Rybolt, Paula Watson, and Sandy Zitkus for their helpful comments, corrections, and suggestions during the preparation of this book. Our thanks also to Ronald I. Perkins of the University of Wisconsin-Madison and to A. M. Sarquis of Miami University, Ohio, for reviewing the manuscript.

DEDICATION

TO OUR MOTHERS, MARIAN MEBANE AND PEGGY RYBOLT
WITH EVERYTHING THERE IS A BEGINNING

ABOUT THE AUTHORS

Robert C. Mebane enjoys going to elementary and middle schools to present chemistry experiments to students. He has a Ph.D. in organic chemistry from Duke University and is a member of the chemistry faculty at the University of Tennessee at Chattanooga. Some of his other interests are backpacking, fishing, and kayaking.

Thomas R. Rybolt has a young daughter who likes to do chemistry experiments with him. He has observed that even young children love to learn about science and the world around them. Dr. Rybolt received his Ph.D. in physical chemistry from Georgia Institute of Technology. He also is a member of the chemistry faculty at the University of Tennessee at Chattanooga.

Doctors Mebane and Rybolt explain why they wrote this book:

> We want to show that the basic ideas of chemistry are simple and beautiful. Many people believe that you need expensive chemicals or computers to learn about chemistry. We've put together experiments using ingredients you can buy in a grocery store. By performing these experiments you learn basic principles of chemistry and have fun learning, too.

CONTENTS

FOREWORD

Chemistry is the central science that lies at the crossroads of physics, biology, and modern technology. Yet it is often ignored at the elementary school level. As far as I know, this well-written book is unique in combining safe, interesting experiments using common everyday materials with an understandable explanation of particles. Although many of the experiments have been used for years, in the past they often have been little more than "magic tricks." The authors of this book have been very skillful in keeping the activities interesting while teaching good science.

The experiments are appropriate for fourth to sixth grades, and many of the activities will appeal as well to middle/junior high school students enrolled in physical science courses. The book is a great teacher resource of home-investigation-type activities. A teacher might assign an investigation and the following day discuss the results with the class. A creative instructor can expand the ideas in the rather simple activities far beyond the explanations given. Because these activities can be readily done at home, this book will also be an important resource for parents who want to interest their children in science, particularly in the field of chemistry.

The book comes at a good time because currently there is a great deal of interest in elementary and middle/junior high school science improvement. The authors have provided an ideal way to support the study of chemistry, both in the elementary and middle/junior high schools and in the home.

Ronald I. Perkins

Assistant Director
Institute for Chemical Education
University of Wisconsin

INTRODUCTION

SCIENCE

Science is an adventure! Science is an adventure of asking questions and finding answers. For thousands of years people have been asking questions about matter, nature, life, and our world. We have learned many wonderful things, but there is much more for us to learn.

Scientists are men and women who ask questions. Scientists answer questions by doing experiments and making observations. Scientists compare the results of their experiments to their ideas and knowledge. The results of their observations increase our knowledge and improve our understanding of the world around us.

Science is exciting because it never stops. There will always be new questions to ask. New questions lead to new experiments. New experiments lead to new knowledge and to new questions.

One way to share in the adventure of science is to do experiments. This book is a collection of experiments which you can do at home or at school. These experiments will help you learn how to ask questions and find answers, and how to become a better observer. As you read about science and do experiments, you will learn more about yourself and your world.

ATOMS, IONS, AND MOLECULES

One of the most important things that scientists have learned about our world is that EVERYTHING IS MADE OF ATOMS. Water, ice, air, sand, table salt, sugar, rocks, shoes, clothes, houses, bicycles, cars, leaves, trees, flowers, bees, ants, spiders, cows, horses, and people are all made of atoms.

Atoms are the basic building blocks of all things. There are 92 different kinds of natural atoms. A few additional atoms have been made by scientists in laboratories. Examples of natural atoms include: oxygen, hydrogen, carbon, nitrogen, mercury, gold, silver, sulfur, helium, chlorine, sodium, neon, nickel, copper, iron, silicon, phosphorus, aluminum, and calcium.

Atoms are found in all things. For example, a piece of aluminum foil is made of aluminum atoms. A diamond consists of carbon atoms. Sand is made of silicon and oxygen atoms. Table sugar is made of carbon, hydrogen, and oxygen atoms.

Atoms are made of smaller particles. These smaller particles are electrons, protons, and neutrons. Electrons are negatively charged and they spin around the nucleus. The nucleus is the center of the atom and contains protons and neutrons. Protons are positively charged and neutrons have no charge.

Atoms and molecules that contain a charge are called ions. Ions have either a positive charge or a negative charge. Positive ions have more protons than electrons. Negative ions have more electrons than protons. Sodium chloride, which is the chemical name for table salt, is made of positive sodium ions and negative chlorine ions.

Atoms or ions combine in chemical reactions to make molecules, metal alloys, or salts. Chemical reactions can also involve changing one molecule into a different molecule or breaking one molecule down into smaller molecules, atoms, or ions.

Molecules are combinations of tightly bound atoms. Water is a combination of hydrogen and oxygen atoms. Imagine you have a drop of water and you divide this drop into smaller and smaller drops. If you could continue to divide the drops enough times, you would eventually end up with a single water molecule. If you divide this water molecule any further, you would have two hydrogen atoms and one oxygen atom.

Scientists use models to represent molecules. The models are made from small balls with the balls representing atoms. These models allow scientists to understand more about molecules. Models of a water molecule, a carbon dioxide molecule, an oxygen molecule, and a methane molecule are shown below. You can make similiar models with marshmallows or gumdrops held together by toothpicks. Each marshmallow or gumdrop can represent one atom.

WATER

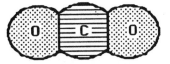

CARBON DIOXIDE

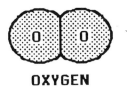

OXYGEN

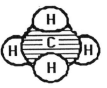

METHANE

A water molecule is a combination of two hydrogen atoms and one oxygen atom. A carbon dioxide molecule is a combination of two oxygen atoms and one carbon atom. An oxygen molecule is a combination of two oxygen atoms. A methane molecule is a combination of four hydrogen atoms and one carbon atom. Natural gas consists of methane molecules.

Molecules that are made of few atoms are very small. Molecules are so small that you cannot see one even with the most powerful microscope. One drop of water contains two million quadrillion (2,000,000,000,000,000,000,000) molecules. If you took two million quadrillion pennies and stacked one on top of the other, you would have three hundred thousand (300,000) stacks of pennies. Each stack would reach from the Sun to Pluto.

If you could magnify one drop of water to the size of the earth, each water molecule would be about the size of an orange.

Polymers are giant molecules made by combining many smaller molecules. Some polymer molecules may contain several million atoms. Important natural polymers include natural rubber, starch, and DNA. Rubber bands and some automobile tires are made of natural rubber. Starch is found in many foods. DNA is the molecule of heredity . Some important polymers made by scientists are nylon, which is used in making fabrics, polyethylene, which is used to make plastic bags and plastic bottles, and polystyrene, which is used in making styrofoam cups and insulation.

ADVENTURES WITH ATOMS AND MOLECULES

This book is a collection of questions and experiments to help you learn more about atoms and molecules. You will discover answers as you do the experiments. You will also find that your answers lead you to ask new questions. Like scientists, you will learn by doing. You will discover that science is not only useful but also fun!

Each experiment is divided into five parts: 1) materials, 2) procedure, 3) observations, 4) discussion, and 5) other things to try. The materials are what you need to do the experiment. The procedure is what you do. The <u>observations</u> are what you see. The <u>discussion</u> explains what your observations tell you about atoms and molecules. The <u>other things to try</u> are additional questions and experiments which you can do to find out more about atoms and molecules.

WHEN YOU DO THESE EXPERIMENTS MAKE SURE YOU

1) Obtain an adult's permission before using anything in your home.

2) Get an adult to watch you when you do an experiment. They en-
   joy seeing experiments too.

3) Follow the directions for each experiment.

4) Clean any glasses or dishes after you use them.

1 DO MOLECULES MOVE?

Materials

Food coloring

A glass of water

Procedure

Set the glass of water on a table. Add one drop of food coloring to the glass of water. Do not move the glass. Watch the color in the water.

FOOD COLORING

IN WATER

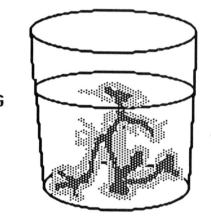

Observations

How does the drop spread out? Does the color move in all directions? Wait until all the water is the color of the food coloring. How long does it take for the water to become completely colored?

Discussion

A molecule is so small that we cannot see one. However, we can see collections of molecules. The water in the glass is a collection of water molecules.

We know that individual molecules move because we can see the collection of food coloring molecules spread thoughout the glass of water. The water is a pale color because each food coloring molecule is surrounded by colorless water molecules.

Molecules are constantly moving. Gas molecules move very fast. Liquid molecules move more slowly. A molecule in a solid only wiggles or vibrates back and forth in one small space.

Other things to try

Open a bottle of vanilla extract. How long does it take before you can smell it? Some of the vanilla extract molecules move from the bottle to your nose. These molecules move through the air faster than the food coloring molecules move through the water.

2 ARE SOME MOLECULES SMALL?

Materials

A balloon

Vanilla extract

Procedure

Pour a small amount of vanilla extract into the balloon. Blow up the balloon. Do not get any vanilla extract in your mouth. Tie off the balloon. Shake the balloon for about thirty seconds.

Observations

Smell the outside of the balloon. Do you smell the vanilla extract? How does it get on the outside of the balloon?

Discussion

<u>Vanillin</u> molecules are found in vanilla extract. Vanillin is a molecule made of eight carbon atoms, eight hydrogen atoms, and three

SMELLING A
BALLOON

oxygen atoms. It is the vanillin molecules that give vanilla extract its taste and smell.

The outside of the balloon smells like vanilla extract because the vanillin molecules pass through the walls of the balloon even though it is closed. There is enough space between the molecules in the balloon to let the vanillin molecules pass through the balloon. Like many molecules vanillin molecules are very small.

Other things to try

Try other smelly things like almond extract or lemon extract to see if they can get out of the balloon.

Blow up a balloon and tie it off with a strong knot. Set the balloon on a shelf and leave it there for three days. What happens to the balloon? Can you explain why the balloon gets smaller?

3 DO HOT MOLECULES MOVE FASTER THAN COLD MOLECULES?

Materials

Food coloring	Tape
A glass of hot water	A felt pen
A glass of cold water	

Procedure

Place a piece of tape on each glass. Write "cold" on one piece of tape and "hot" on the other. Fill the glass labeled "cold" with cold water from a sink faucet. Fill the glass labeled "hot" with hot water from a sink faucet. Make sure the water is hot. Set each glass on a table. Add one drop of food coloring to each glass of water. Do not move the glasses. Watch the color in each glass.

Observations

Watch the color spread out in each glass. Which one spreads out faster? When the hot water is an even, pale color, look at the cold water. Is the cold water an even color yet?

Discussion

Molecules are always moving. The food coloring molecules spread out through the water. This type of movement is called diffusion. The diffusion of the food coloring molecules makes the water take on an even color.

The hot water becomes colored faster than the cold water. Hot molecules move faster than cold molecules. A hot pie has a stronger smell than a cold pie because molecules from the hot pie move faster and move into the air more quickly.

FOOD COLORING
IN

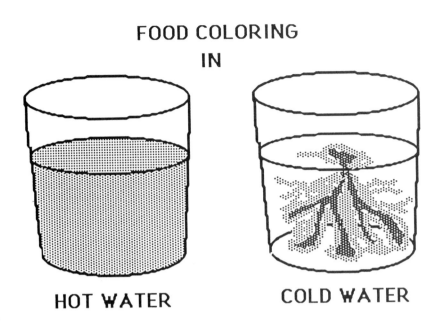

HOT WATER   COLD WATER

Other things to try

Put a tea bag in a glass of hot water. Put another tea bag in a glass of cold water. Why does the hot water get darker first?

Put a drop of food coloring in a glass of cold water. Put a drop of food coloring in a second glass of cold water. Stir the water in the second glass with a spoon. This water gets colored faster because you have moved the molecules with the spoon. Do you have a better understanding of why we stir drinks?

Put a drop of food coloring on a piece of ice. Why doesn't the food coloring move into the ice? In the solid ice, the molecules are wiggling, but they don't move past each other. The food coloring molecules cannot move through the solid. Have you ever tried to walk through a crowd of people when everyone else is standing still? It is much easier to get through the crowd if all the people are moving. It is much easier for molecules to move through a liquid than through a solid.

4 IS THERE SPACE BETWEEN SUGAR CRYSTALS?

Materials

Hot tap water   A one-cup measuring cup

Sugar   A two-cup measuring cup

A spoon

Procedure

Put one cup of hot tap water in the two-cup measuring cup. Add one-half cup of sugar to the hot water. Stir the water with a spoon until the sugar dissolves. You can no longer see the sugar when it dissolves.

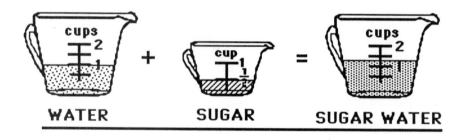

WATER   SUGAR   SUGAR WATER

Observations

How long does it take for the sugar to dissolve? How much liquid is in the two-cup measure after the sugar has dissolved?

Discussion

In this experiment one-half cup of sugar is dissolved in one cup of water. You might think that you should have one-and-a-half cups of sugar water in the measuring cup. However, there is less than one-and-a-half cups of sugar water in the measuring cup.

The major reason why there is less sugar water than expected is because there is space between the sugar crystals in the one-half cup measure. This space is occupied by air. When the sugar crystals dissolve in the water the sugar molecules, which make up the sugar crystals, are surrounded by water molecules. Small molecules of sugar and water will fit closer together than large sugar crystals.

Another reason why there is less sugar water in the measuring cup is because when the sugar crystals dissolve in the water, the sugar molecules go into the empty spaces between the water molecules. There are spaces between molecules in a liquid.

Other things to try

Repeat this experiment with table salt. Do you get the same results? Try other things such as sand, baking soda, and flour. What results do you get?

5 ARE GAS MOLECULES FARTHER APART THAN LIQUID MOLECULES?

Materials

Two small, identical, unopened bottles of Coke

(Coke is a registered trademark of the Coca-Cola Company)

A balloon

A bottle opener

A pan of hot water

Procedure

Use hot water from your sink faucet to fill a pan. Open one of the bottles of Coke. Quickly slip a balloon over the top of the bottle. Shake the bottle with the balloon over it. Set this bottle in the pan of hot water. NEVER HEAT A BOTTLE COVERED WITH ANYTHING OTHER THAN A BALLOON.

Observations

Does the balloon get bigger? Do you see bubbles of gas in the bottle? Is the balloon filling up with gas?

Wait until the balloon stops getting bigger. Set the two bottles next to each other. Look at the amount of Coke in each bottle. Is the amount of liquid in each bottle about the same?

Discussion

Coke is a carbonated drink. A <u>carbonated</u> <u>drink</u> is one which has carbon dioxide molecules in it. The bubbles you see when you open a Coke are bubbles of carbon dioxide gas that are leaving the liquid. As long as the bottle is not opened the carbon dioxide stays in the liquid.

When the carbon dioxide molecules are in the Coke, they are surrounded by water molecules. When you open a bottle or can of Coke,

OPENED BOTTLE   **CLOSED BOTTLE**

some of the carbon dioxide molecules escape from the liquid as a gas. Your balloon gets bigger because it is being filled with carbon dioxide gas. The amount of liquid only decreases a little after you open the bottle. However, the balloon gets much larger. The carbon dioxide gas molecules are much farther apart than the liquid molecules.

Gas molecules are so far apart that most of the space in the balloon is empty. The balloon stays large because the gas molecules inside are in constant motion. The molecules are constantly hitting each other and the inside of the balloon.

Other things to try

Try this same experiment with different carbonated drinks. Do some drinks have more carbon dioxide gas in them than others?

Open a bottle and cover it with a balloon. Put this bottle in the refrigerator. Open a second bottle and put it in a pan of hot water. The balloon on the bottle in the refrigerator should not get as large as the balloon on the bottle in the hot water. The cold temperature makes the molecules move slower and they are less likely to leave the liquid. We cap carbonated drinks and then put them in the refrigerator to keep them from losing carbon dioxide gas.

6 IS A GAS MADE BY MIXING VINEGAR AND BAKING SODA?

Materials

Baking soda	A teaspoon
Vinegar	A measuring cup
A balloon	An empty soft drink bottle

Procedure

Place one-half teaspoon of baking soda in the empty soft drink bottle. Add one-quarter cup of vinegar to the soft drink bottle. Quickly place a balloon on the neck of the bottle. Carefully shake the bottle to mix the vinegar and the baking soda. Set the bottle on a table and make your observations.

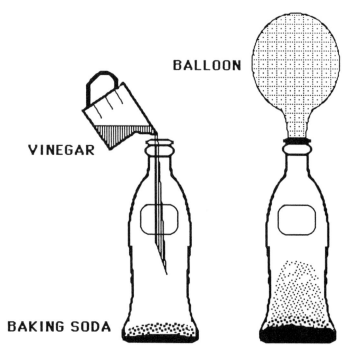

BALLOON

VINEGAR

BAKING SODA

Observations

Do you see bubbles when you add the vinegar to the baking soda? Do the bubbles rise in the bottle? How long does it take for the bubbles to stop forming in the bottle? What happens to the balloon when you put it on the bottle? Does shaking the bottle cause more bubbles to form? Does the balloon get larger when you shake the bottle?

Discussion

Baking soda is a chemical called <u>sodium</u> <u>bicarbonate</u>. <u>Vinegar</u> is water that contains a small amount of a chemical called <u>acetic</u> <u>acid</u>. When vinegar is mixed with baking soda, a chemical reaction occurs.

In this experiment the chemical reaction between the sodium bicarbonate and the acetic acid makes <u>carbon dioxide</u> molecules. Carbon dioxide molecules are a gas. We cannot see the gas. We know that a gas is formed in the reaction because the balloon catches the gas and gets larger.

Carbon dioxide gas molecules made in this chemical reaction move throughout the bottle and into the balloon. When the bottle is shaken, the baking soda and the vinegar mix. This mixing causes a faster reaction and more gas is produced. This is why the balloon becomes larger when the bottle is shaken.

Other things to try

Use lemon, grapefruit, or lime juice instead of vinegar in this experiment. Does the chemical reaction between juice and baking soda make a gas?

Open a carbonated drink and quickly place a balloon over the top of the bottle. Is a gas produced when you open a carbonated drink?

How can you show that a gas is not produced when table salt is added to water?

17

7 ARE SOME MOLECULES HEAVIER THAN OTHERS?

Materials

Baking soda	A meter stick or yardstick
Vinegar	Two grocery bags
A large plastic pail	Five pieces of string

Procedure

A balance can be used to measure weights. Make a balance like the one shown. Tie a paper bag to each end of a meter stick. Tie another string in the middle of the meter stick and have a friend hold the string. Move the string along the stick until you get the bags balanced at the same height from the floor.

You need to make some carbon dioxide molecules. Cover the bottom of the plastic pail with one cup of baking soda. Next pour two cups of

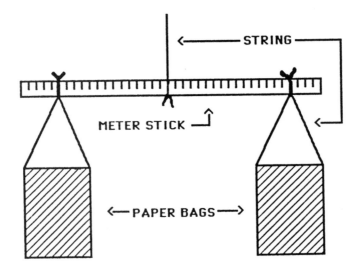

vinegar into the pail. You will see bubbles of carbon dioxide gas form. Wait about thirty seconds. Now tilt the pail above one bag so the carbon dioxide gas is poured out of the pail and into the bag. DO NOT POUR ANY LIQUID INTO THE BAG.

When you have finished making your observations, pour the liquid in the pail down the sink. Rinse the pail and the sink with water.

Observations

Which paper bag went down - the one containing the air molecules or the one containing the carbon dioxide molecules? Continue to hold the balance steady for several minutes. Do both paper bags move back to the same height?

Discussion

Air is made of mostly nitrogen and oxygen molecules and a small amount of carbon dioxide molecules. Carbon dioxide molecules weigh more than air molecules. Originally there are only air molecules in both bags. When the carbon dioxide gas is poured into one of the bags the carbon dioxide molecules replace the air molecules. The bag containing the carbon dioxide molecules moves down.

The paper bags move back to their original position after several minutes because the carbon dioxide molecules move out of the bag and into the room. Only air molecules are left in both paper bags.

Other things to try

Why does a balloon filled with helium go up in the air? Which is heavier - helium or air?

8 ARE MOLECULES ATTRACTED BY CHARGES?

Materials

Two paper cups	A measuring cup
Water	A plastic ballpoint pen
Cooking oil	A bowl

Procedure

Punch a small hole about the size of a pencil lead in the bottom of each cup with the tip of a ballpoint pen. Cover the tip of the pen with a cap.

Cover the small hole of one of the cups with your finger. While holding the cup over the sink add about one-quarter cup of water to it. Rub the covered plastic ballpoint pen in your hair or on a sweater for about thirty seconds. Uncover the hole to allow a stream of water to flow. Move the middle of the ballpoint pen close to the thin stream of water, but do not touch the stream.

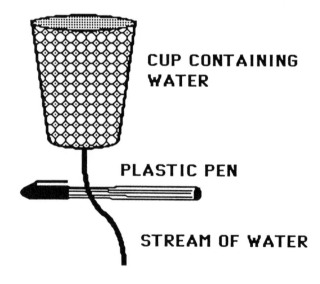

CUP CONTAINING WATER

PLASTIC PEN

STREAM OF WATER

When you finish making your observations with the water, repeat the experiment with cooking oil. Place a bowl in the sink to catch the stream of cooking oil. Put about one-quarter cup of cooking oil in the second cup. Rub the covered ballpoint pen in your hair or on a sweater. Move the pen close to the thin stream of cooking oil.

Observations

Is the thin stream of water bent by the plastic ballpoint pen? Does the stream of water move towards the pen? How close does the pen have to be to see the stream of water bend? Is the stream of water bent more as you move the pen closer to the stream? What happens when you touch the pen to the stream of water? Is the thin stream of cooking oil bent by the plastic pen?

Discussion

A water molecule is made of two hydrogen atoms and one oxygen atom. The combination of hydrogen and oxygen atoms in water makes water molecules polar. A polar molecule has two ends like a magnet. One end has a positive charge. The other end has a negative charge.

Oil molecules are made of mostly carbon and hydrogen atoms. Oil molecules are nonpolar. A nonpolar molecule does not have a positive and negative end. Nonpolar molecules are called neutral molecules.

When the plastic ballpoint pen is rubbed in your hair or on a sweater, negative charges are rubbed onto the plastic pen. These negative charges are called electrons. The plastic pen becomes negatively charged. When the negatively charged pen is moved close to a stream of water, the negative charges on the pen attract the positive end of the water molecules. The stream of water moves towards the plastic pen because positive charges and negative charges attract each other. Objects with the same charge repel each other.

The stream of oil is not moved by the charged plastic pen. Oil molecules are not attracted or repelled by the charged plastic pen because oil molecules do not have charges.

Other things to try

Use other plastic things to bend the water. A plastic comb will work. Do some plastic objects move the stream of water more than others?

Rub a balloon in your hair or on a sweater. Does the charged balloon move the stream of water?

Does the stream of water still bend towards the charged plastic ballpoint pen when salt is dissolved in water?

Rub the covered pen on a piece of cotton. Does the pen still bend the water? Try rubbing other materials to see if you can rub electrons off of them.

DO SIMILAR MOLECULES ATTRACT EACH OTHER?

Materials

A large piece of wax paper

Water

Cooking oil

Procedure

Put two drops of water about the size of dimes next to each other on the wax paper. Slowly move the drops together until they touch. You can move a drop by slowly lifting one side of the wax paper. You can also move a drop by dragging a paper clip through it.

Repeat this experiment using oil. Put two drops of oil next to each other on the wax paper. Move the drops together so they touch each other.

Repeat this experiment again using water and oil. Put a drop of water and a drop of oil on the wax paper. Move them together.

Observations

When the two drops of water touch, do they go together to make one big drop? When the two drops of oil touch, do they go together to make one big drop? When the drop of oil and water touch, do they go together to make one big drop?

Discussion

The water drops go together to make a bigger water drop. The oil drops go together to make a bigger oil drop. The oil and water drop will not go together to make a bigger drop. The oil and water will not go together because they are not made of similar molecules.

Do you know that like molecules attract like molecules? Another way of saying this is that polar molecules attract polar molecules, and nonpolar molecules attract nonpolar molecules. <u>Polar</u> molecules have a negative side and a positive side. <u>Nonpolar</u> molecules do not have a positive and negative side. Water molecules are polar. Oil molecules are nonpolar.

The two water drops jumped together when they touched because they are both made of polar molecules. The two oil drops jumped together when they touched because they are both made of nonpolar molecules.

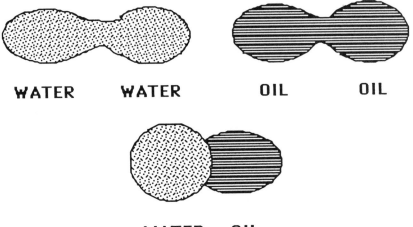

WATER   WATER   OIL   OIL

WATER   OIL

The water drop and the oil drop will not go together because the water is polar and the oil is nonpolar.

Other things to try

Put ten drops of water on a piece of wax paper. Can you collect them together in one big drop by moving one drop around to collect the others?

Put a drop of oil and a drop of water on a piece of wax paper. Tilt the wax paper so the drops run down the paper. Does the oil drop spread out in a thin layer? Does the water stay together in a drop? Does the oil drop move more slowly than a water drop? The nonpolar oil is attracted to the nonpolar wax paper so it spreads out. The attraction between the oil drop and the wax paper makes the oil drop move more slowly than the water drop. The polar water is not attracted to the nonpolar wax paper so it stays in a drop.

10 CAN STRETCHING MOLECULES MAKE THEM GIVE OFF HEAT?

Materials

A large flat rubber band (about one-quarter inch wide)

Procedure

Touch the rubber band to your forehead. Your forehead is very sensitive to temperature. This will give you an idea of the temperature of the rubber band before you stretch it. The rubber band should feel a little cooler than your forehead.

Pinch the rubber band between the thumb and index finger of your left hand. With the thumb and index finger of your right hand, pinch the rubber band at a point right next to your left hand. Make sure your thumbs are touching each other. You want to have only a little bit of rubber band to stretch.

Quickly pull your hands apart. Stretch the small amount of rubber band between your fingers as far as you can, but do not break the rubber band. While the rubber band is still stretched, quickly touch the stretched part of the rubber band to your forehead.

Let the rubber band go back to its regular size. Move your hands and touch the rubber band to your forehead.

Observations

Does the rubber band feel warmer when it is stretched? Does the temperature return to its original temperature when the rubber band is not stretched?

Discussion

In this experiment you are changing work to heat. <u>Work</u> is the energy of directed motion. Riding a bicycle, pushing a weight, and

26

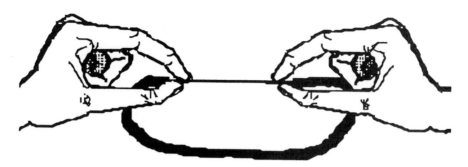

STRETCHING A RUBBER BAND

stretching a rubber band are examples of directed motion. These activities take work.

Heat is the energy of random motion of molecules. When you heat water on a stove you make the molecules of water move faster. However, the molecules are moving in all different directions. When a solid gets hotter its molecules vibrate more rapidly.

The rubber band is made of coiled molecules. When you stretch the rubber band the coiled molecules are straightened. When you release the rubber band the molecules return to their coiled shapes.

When you stretch the rubber band you change work energy into heat energy. The rubber band feels warm when you touch it to your forehead. When you let the rubber band go, it returns to its normal shape and it no longer feels warm.

Other things to try

Try rubbing your hands back and forth against each other. They will soon get hot. You have converted work to heat.

Try pulling the rubber band over and over. It should get hot each time it is stretched.

Try some other things that can be stretched to see if they get hot. You can use a balloon or the plastic used to hold a six-pack of soft drink cans together.

11 CAN MOLECULES BE BROKEN INTO SMALLER MOLECULES?

Materials

Yeast	A tablespoon
Warm water	A teaspoon
Sugar	A measuring cup
A glass	

Procedure

Fill a glass with one-half cup of warm water. Add one teaspoon of sugar. Stir until the sugar dissolves. Sugar seems to disappear when it dissolves because sugar molecules are surrounded by water molecules. Now add one tablespoon or one package of yeast to the glass. Stir for about a minute to dissolve the yeast. Set the glass in the sink.

WATER AND SUGAR   WATER, SUGAR
AND YEAST

After you have made your observations, pour the yeast mixture down the drain. Rinse the glass and the sink with water.

Observations

What color is the yeast mixture? Can you smell the yeast? Do you see bubbles forming in the glass? How long does it take to see the first bubbles? Does the yeast mixture get larger?

Discussion

Enzymes are complex molecules made by living organisms. Enzymes are found in the cells of the living organisms. Your body is made of trillions of cells. There are many enzymes in each cell. These enzymes cause specific chemical reactions in cells.

Yeast is a simple living organism called a fungus. Yeast cells contain many different enzymes. One enzyme in yeast cells causes the breakdown of sugar molecules into carbon dioxide molecules and ethyl alcohol molecules.

Sugar molecules are larger than carbon dioxide molecules and ethyl alcohol molecules. The breakdown of sugar molecules is a chemical reaction called fermentation. Yeast cells obtain energy to grow from the fermentation of sugar molecules. The yeast mixture gets larger because of the carbon dioxide gas produced.

The carbon dioxide that is produced during the fermentation is a gas. You can see the carbon dioxide gas bubbles in the yeast mixture. Yeast is used in baking to make breads rise. Yeast makes carbon dioxide gas from the sugar. The gas is trapped in the dough. When the bread is baked the carbon dioxide gas bubbles get larger. These bubbles make holes in the dough. These holes make the bread lighter and tastier.

Other things to try

Repeat the experiment using two teaspoons of sugar. Do you see more carbon dioxide bubbles? When you use more sugar, you should see more carbon dioxide bubbles.

Add a tablespoon or one package of yeast to one cup of warm water. Are carbon dioxide molecules made? Are there as many carbon dioxide bubbles made as there were when sugar was added to the yeast?

CAN DIFFERENT MOLECULES BE SEPARATED FROM EACH OTHER? **12**

Materials

A small bowl   Scissors

A paper towel   Water

Green food coloring

Procedure

Cut a strip of paper towel about nine inches long and two inches wide. Place a drop of food coloring about three inches from one end of the strip. Dip the end nearest the spot in a bowl of water. Leave about a half an inch of the strip in the water. Let the remaining strip hang over the bowl into a sink. Do not let the food coloring spot get in the water.

BOWL OF WATER

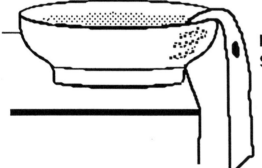

FOOD COLORING SPOT

STRIP OF PAPER TOWEL

Observations

Does the water move along the paper towel? Does the water move as a line? What happens when the water line reaches the spot? Does the water line pass through the spot? Does the spot move with the water?

Do you see the spot separating into different colors? How many colors do you see? Do some colors move farther than others? How long did it take for the water to reach the end of the paper towel?

Discussion

A <u>mixture</u> is a combination of several different things. For example, if you mix red marbles and blue marbles you have a mixture of different colored marbles. To separate this mixture of marbles you can pick out all the red marbles and place them in a separate pile.

Separating a mixture of molecules is not as easy as separating different colored marbles. Chemists have developed many ways to separate a mixture of molecules. The technique used in this experiment is called <u>chromatography</u>. Chromatography means color writing.

To separate different molecules by chromatography, the mixture of molecules is first placed on a material called the <u>adsorbent</u>. The molecules stick to the adsorbent. In this experiment, paper is the adsorbent. The mixture of molecules is the food coloring. The different molecules in the mixture separate from each other when a liquid flows through the adsorbent. The liquid is called a <u>solvent</u>. The solvent in this experiment is water.

Some of the molecules are strongly attracted by the water. The attracted molecules move with the water. Other molecules are only slightly attracted by the water. These molecules are attracted more to the paper. Therefore they do not move as far as do the molecules which are attracted by the water. When you do this experiment, molecules are separated and you see several colors on the paper towel.

Other things to try

Try different food colorings. Which food coloring separates into the most colors? Which food coloring separates into the least number of colors?

Try separating the colors in felt-tipped pens. This can be done by coloring a circle about the size of a dime with the felt-tipped pen on a strip of paper towel and then placing the strip in the bowl of water as before.

13 CAN THE FLAVOR OF APPLES BE ISOLATED FROM APPLE CIDER VINEGAR?

Materials

Two paper cups	A measuring cup
Apple cider vinegar	Tape
Distilled white vinegar	A felt pen

Procedure

Put a piece of tape on each cup. Use the felt pen to label one cup "apple cider vinegar" and the other cup "distilled vinegar." Make sure to write on the tape.

Pour one-quarter cup of apple cider vinegar into the paper cup labeled "apple cider vinegar." Pour one-quarter cup of distilled white vinegar in the paper cup labeled "distilled vinegar." Place the cups in a warm spot for several days. A windowsill that gets plenty of sun is a good place to set the cups. Smell the liquid in the cups each day. Sometimes a little mold will form in the cups, but it will not affect the experiment.

Observations

What color is the apple cider vinegar? What color is the distilled white vinegar? What does the apple cider vinegar smell like? Does the distilled white vinegar have the same smell as the apple cider vinegar?

How many days does it take for the liquid in each cup to disappear? Is there a sticky brown substance left in the cup which contained the apple cider vinegar? Does this brown sticky substance smell like vinegar? Does this brown sticky substance smell like apples? Is there anything left in the cup that contained the distilled white vinegar?

Discussion

Vinegar is a sour liquid which can be made from many things. Apple cider vinegar is made from apples. Distilled white vinegar is usually made from grains like wheat or corn. The first step in making vinegar is the fermentation of the sugars in the apples or the grains. Fermentation produces an alcohol called ethanol.

Acetic acid is the substance that makes vinegar sour. Vinegar is a mixture of water and acetic acid. A chemical reaction turns ethanol molecules into acetic acid molecules. In this reaction two hydrogen atoms are removed and one oxygen atom is added to each ethanol molecule.

Vinegar made from apples contains the molecules that give apples their flavor and color. These flavor molecules usually cannot be smelled in the vinegar because the acetic acid has a stronger smell. The flavor molecules of apples can, however, be isolated from apple cider vinegar.

In this experiment the acetic acid molecules and the water molecules are removed by evaporation. In evaporation, liquid molecules are changed into gas molecules. Heat helps speed up the conversion of liquid molecules into gas molecules. This is why vinegar evaporates when placed in a warm spot.

When the acetic acid and the water molecules evaporate, some of the apple flavor molecules are left. The apple flavor molecules are in the brown, sticky substance in the bottom of the cup that contained the apple cider vinegar. This brown, sticky substance is called a residue. It is expected that there will not be a residue in the cup that contained the distilled white vinegar. The flavor molecules from the grain are

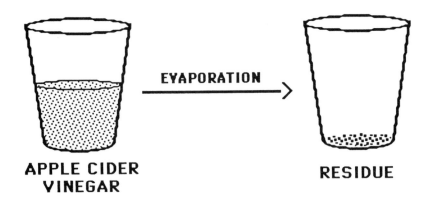

APPLE CIDER
VINEGAR

EVAPORATION

RESIDUE

usually removed before the vinegar is put in the bottle, so there is nothing from which to make a residue.

Other things to try

Can you isolate the flavor molecules from tea? Make a cup of tea and let it sit in a warm place until all the water is gone. What does the residue smell like?

Can you isolate table salt from a cup of salt water? How would you do this?

ARE RUBBER MOLECULES LESS BOUNCY WHEN COLD?   **14**

Materials

Two identical rubber balls

A refrigerator freezer

Procedure

Find two rubber balls that bounce to about the same height. Put one ball in the freezer section of a refrigerator. Leave the other ball out in the room. Wait about four hours.

Take the ball out of the freezer. Stand on a hard floor. Hold a ball in each hand. Hold your arms straight out and drop both balls. Drop both balls several more times.

Observations

Which ball bounces higher? How high does the colder ball bounce? How high does the warmer ball bounce? Does the warmer ball still bounce after the cold ball stops? Count the number of bounces for each ball.

Discussion

A rubber molecule is a special type of molecule called a polymer. Polymer molecules are made of thousands of smaller molecules. The smaller molecules are joined together to make long chains. One long chain makes a single polymer molecule.

Some polymers are very rigid and stiff, like a plastic bottle. Other polymers are very flexible and can be stretched like a rubber band. Long chains of rubber molecules in a rubber ball can be pushed together

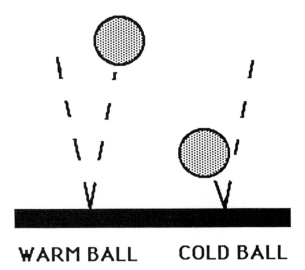

WARM BALL   COLD BALL

or pulled apart. The ability of these molecules to be pushed and pulled is what makes a rubber ball bouncy.

When rubber becomes cold, the molecules change from being flexible and stretchy to being stiff and rigid. When this happens, they cannot snap back into position. When a rubber ball gets very cold it will not bounce very high.

Other things to try

Let the cold ball get warm. Does it bounce high again?

Repeat this experiment with other types of balls. Try tennis balls, golf balls, or racquetballs. You can try this experiment outside if it is a very cold day (20 degrees Fahrenheit or colder).

WILL AIR MOLECULES FLOAT ON CARBON DIOXIDE MOLECULES? 15

Materials

Baking soda	A measuring cup
Vinegar	Soap bubble liquid and ring
Kitchen sink	

You can buy a bottle of soap bubble mix in toy stores and in many grocery stores, or you can mix dishwashing liquid with water to make your own soap bubble mix. Soap bubble kits come with a ring to blow bubbles. You can make your own ring from a piece of wire. Bend the wire to make a small loop.

Procedure

Sprinkle one-and-a-half cups of baking soda evenly over the bottom of the kitchen sink. Pour two cups of vinegar on the baking soda. Blow soap bubbles into the sink.

Rinse the sink with water after you have finished the experiment.

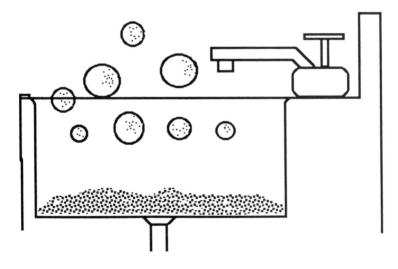

Observations

What happens when the vinegar is added to the baking soda? How long does the baking soda and the vinegar mixture fizz? Do the soap bubbles float to the bottom of the sink? Do large soap bubbles come to rest at the same level as the smaller soap bubbles? After a while, do the soap bubbles drop to the bottom of the sink? How long does it take for the bubbles to drop to the bottom of the sink? Will bubbles still float in the sink after one minute?

Discussion

When the vinegar is added to the baking soda, a chemical reaction occurs. This chemical reaction produces molecules of carbon dioxide gas. Carbon dioxide molecules are heavier than air molecules. Air is mostly nitrogen and oxygen molecules. In this experiment we see that soap bubbles are lighter than carbon dioxide gas.

The soap bubbles are made of soap and water molecules, and are filled with air molecules. When a soap bubble is blown into the sink, it cannot reach the bottom of the sink since the air molecules in the bubble are lighter than carbon dioxide molecules. The soap bubble floats on the carbon dioxide gas.

Other things to try

Put one-fourth cup of baking soda in the sink. Add one-half cup of vinegar to the baking soda. Is enough carbon dioxide gas made to float soap bubbles?

What is the least amount of vinegar that must be mixed with one-and-a-half cups of baking soda to make enough carbon dioxide gas to float soap bubbles?

ARE THERE WATER MOLECULES IN THE AIR? **16**

Materials

A dry glass

Ice cubes

Water

Procedure

Fill a dry glass with ice cubes. Then pour water into the glass until it is almost full. Be careful not to get any water on the outside of the glass.

Observations

Wait about ten minutes and then feel the outside of the glass. Does it feel wet? Can you see small drops of water on the glass? How long did it take for water droplets to appear on the outside of the glass? Why is there water on the outside of the glass? Where do the water droplets come from?

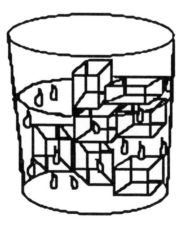

ICE WATER

Discussion

Air is made of nitrogen, oxygen, and carbon dioxide molecules. There are also gaseous water molecules in the air. All of the molecules in the air are constantly moving. Usually they bounce off anything they hit. However, when the water molecules in the air hit the side of the cold glass, they cool off and stick to it.

The water molecules that stick on the glass are changed from a gas to a liquid. The other molecules in the air will not stick to the glass. The glass is not cold enough for nitrogen, oxygen, or carbon dioxide to change into liquids.

Other things to try

Do you know that the clouds in the sky are made of small drops of water? You can make a cloud of water drops. Go outside on a very cold day and blow into the air. Do you see a white cloud? The warm gaseous water in your breath is changed to small drops of cold, liquid water.

Look at a mirror in a bathroom after you take a hot shower. Is there water on the mirror? How did it get there?

Frost is frozen water or ice. Can you explain how frost gets on a car window in the winter?

DO SOAP MOLECULES SPREAD OUT ON THE SURFACE OF WATER?   **17**

Materials

A plate	Dishwashing liquid
Water	Pepper

Procedure

Pour water into a plate until it is full of water. Sprinkle pepper all over the surface of the water. Drop one drop of dishwashing liquid into the center of the plate containing the pepper. Watch the pepper.

Observations

What happens to the pepper? Does all the pepper get pushed to the outside of the plate?

PEPPER ON WATER

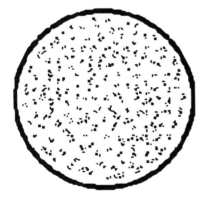 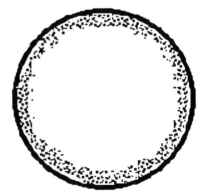

BEFORE SOAP ADDED   **AFTER SOAP ADDED**

Discussion

Soap molecules are made of a short, polar end and a long, nonpolar end. The polar end is attracted to water. The nonpolar end is not attracted to water.

When soap is dropped on the surface of water, it spreads out over the surface. The polar end goes in the water. The long nonpolar end sticks up in the air. As the soap molecules spread out over the surface, the pepper is pushed out of the way. The pepper is pushed to the edge of the plate.

Other things to try

You can repeat this experiment with other things that float on water. You can try chili powder, cinnamon, oregano leaves, or parsley. The spreading soap will push anything on the surface to the side of the plate.

Add several drops of soap to a cup of water. Stir this mixture until you have soapy water. Drop one drop of this mixture onto the pepper floating on the plate of water. The pepper will spread out some, but not all the way to the edge of the plate. There are enough soap molecules to cover part, but not all, of the surface. As you add more drops, the pepper spreads out farther.

DO WATER MOLECULES AND OIL MOLECULES 18 MIX?

Materials

Cooking oil   A measuring cup
Water   A tall, slender jar with a tight-fitting lid
Dishwashing liquid   A tablespoon

Procedure

Pour one cup of water and one tablespoon of cooking oil into the jar. Attach the jar lid. Shake the jar to mix the oil and water. Set the jar on a table. Observe the jar for several minutes.

Add one tablespoon of dishwashing liquid to the jar. Shake the jar for about a minute. Set the jar on a table. Observe the jar for several minutes.

Observations

Do oil and water mix? Which layer is the oil? Which layer is the water? Which is heavier, oil or water?

WATER AND OIL

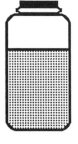
WATER, OIL AND SOAP

Can you see through the two layers in the jar? What happens to the oil and water when you shake the jar. Do the oil and water separate back into two layers? What happens to the oil when you add the dishwashing liquid and then shake the jar? Can you see through the jar now? Is the mixture cloudy? Is the mixture colored?

Discussion

A water molecule is made of two hydrogen atoms and one oxygen atom. This combination of atoms makes water molecules polar. There are two ends to a water molecule. One end has a negative charge and the other end has a positive charge.

Oil molecules are made of mostly carbon and hydrogen atoms. This combination of atoms makes oil nonpolar. Nonpolar means there are no charges on the molecules.

Molecules that are polar will mix with each other. Molecules that are nonpolar will mix with each other. However, polar molecules and nonpolar molecules will not mix with each other. Scientists say that like molecules dissolve like molecules. Oil and water do not mix because water is polar and oil is nonpolar.

Soap molecules are very interesting because they are polar and nonpolar. A soap molecule is long. One end of the molecule is polar and the other end is nonpolar. When soap is added to water and oil, the nonpolar end of the soap molecule mixes with the nonpolar oil. The polar end of the soap molecule mixes with the polar water. This combination of polar and nonpolar molecules causes the mixture to be cloudy. Do you understand now why we use soaps and detergents to clean greasy messes?

Other Things to Try

Pour one cup of water and one tablespoon of cooking oil into a tall, slender jar. Can you show that the large layer on the bottom is water by adding a couple of drops of water? The drops of water will pass through the oil layer.

Try different types of soaps and oils. Do you get the same results?

Try adding just a little soap to the water and oil. What happens?

Does sugar dissolve in oil? Does table salt dissolve in oil?

19 ARE SOME LIQUIDS MORE DENSE THAN OTHERS?

Materials

Corn syrup	A measuring cup
Cooking oil	Several colors of food coloring
Water	A tall, clear drinking glass
A tablespoon	

Procedure

Color one-quarter cup of corn syrup red by stirring one drop of red food coloring into the syrup. Color one-quarter cup of water blue with one drop of blue food coloring.

Add one-quarter cup of cooking oil to a tall, clear glass. Tilt the glass and slowly pour the blue water down the side of the glass. With the glass still tilted, slowly pour the red corn syrup down the side of the glass. Set the glass on a table.

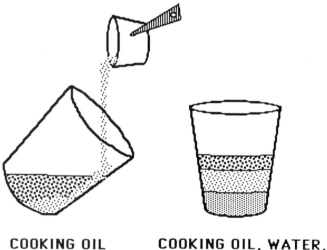

COOKING OIL
AND WATER

COOKING OIL, WATER,
AND CORN SYRUP

After you have made your observations, pour the liquids in the glass down the drain and rinse the glass and sink with warm water and a little detergent.

Observations

What color is the cooking oil? Does the blue water sink through the oil and rest on the bottom of the glass? Does any of the blue water mix with the oil layer? Does the red corn syrup pass through the oil layer? Does the yellow corn syrup pass through the blue water layer? Does the corn syrup mix with the oil or the water? How many layers do you see?

Discussion

The same volumes of two liquids may have different weights. The heavier liquid has a greater <u>density</u>. A liquid that is less dense than water will float on water. A liquid that is more dense than water will sink to the bottom of a glass of water.

In this experiment we use a liquid that is more dense than water and another one that is less dense than water. Corn syrup sinks to the bottom because it is more dense than water. Cooking oil floats on water because it is less dense than water.

Food coloring is used to help you see the different layers. The colors do not change the densities of the liquids.

Other things to try

Try adding the three liquids in different orders. Does changing the order change the final positions of the liquids in the glass?

Add a drop of water to the glass containing the three liquid layers. Which layer does the drop mix with?

Dissolve two tablespoons of salt in one-quarter cup of water. Add this to the glass containing the three layers. Does the salt water layer pass through all the layers? Which liquids are less dense than the salt water?

Take a teaspoon of corn syrup and color it green with food coloring. Add a drop of this green syrup to the glass. What happens to the drop of green corn syrup when it is added to the glass containing the three layers?

DOES HARD WATER CLEAN AS WELL AS SOFT WATER? 20

Materials

Two jars with lids   A tablespoon

Warm water   A measuring cup

Ivory Soap   Epsom salt

(Ivory Soap is a registered trademark of Procter and Gamble)

Procedure

ASK AN ADULT TO HELP YOU CUT TWO PIECES OF SOAP ABOUT THE SIZE OF A PEA FROM A BAR OF IVORY SOAP. Ivory Soap is used because it is pure soap.

Fill each jar with one-half cup of warm water. Place a small piece of Ivory Soap in each jar. Add one tablespoon of Epsom salt to one of the jars. Attach the jar lids. Shake the jars for one minute.

The water in some parts of the country is harder than in other areas. If you do not get any suds with your water and one piece of soap, your tap water may be hard. If your tap water is hard, you will need to add several pieces of soap to each jar.

Observations

Are there suds in the jar containing the Epsom salt? Are there suds in the jar containing just the soap? Are there more suds in the jar containing just the soap? Is the water in the jar containing the Epsom salt cloudy? Is there solid material in the jar containing the Epsom salt? How long does it take for the suds in each jar to disappear?

Discussion

Soap molecules contain a long nonpolar end and a small polar end. The polar end contains a negative charge. The nonpolar end of soap mixes with oil, fat, and grease because they are nonpolar. The polar end of soap mixes with water since water is polar.

Soap cleans by breaking large oil drops into small drops. These small drops of oil dissolve in water. Small drops of soap and oil can be washed away with water.

Hard water makes it more difficult for soap to break oil drops into smaller drops. Hard water contains ions. Ions are atoms or groups of atoms that contain a positive or negative charge. Hard water contains positive ions of magnesium, calcium, or iron. Any of these ions can make water hard. Soft water does not contain these ions.

In this experiment hard water is made by dissolving Epsom salt in water. Epsom salt contains magnesium ions.

Soap molecules do not dissolve in hard water. When soap is added to hard water, the positive ions in the water stick to the negative charge on the polar ends of the soap molecules. A white, waxy solid forms.

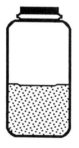 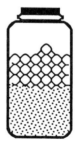

SOAP, WATER AND MAGNESIUM IONS   **SOAP AND WATER**

Bathtub rings are made of this white, waxy solid. Since soap does not dissolve in hard water, there are few suds.

If the positive ions that make water hard are removed, then the water becomes soft. Soft water is better for cleaning. The process of removing the ions that make water hard is called <u>water softening</u>.

Other things to try

Do the experiment again using a clothes or dishwashing detergent. You should see suds even in the hard water with the detergent. The positive ions in hard water do not change detergent molecules as much as they change soap molecules.

Add a teaspoon of table salt (sodium chloride) to some water and see if you can make suds with a piece of Ivory Soap. Add a teaspoon of sugar and see if you can make suds. Table salt and sugar do not make water hard.

Add a tablespoon of vinegar to one-half cup of water in a jar containing a piece of Ivory Soap. Attach the lid and shake. Do you see suds? If you do not, it is because the vinegar contains positive ions which prevent soap molecules from dissolving in water.

21 CAN SALT KEEP WATER FROM FREEZING?

Materials

Two paper cups	A refrigerator freezer
A one-cup measuring cup	Salt
A teaspoon	Tape
Water	A felt pen

Procedure

Put a piece of tape on each cup. Use the felt pen to label one cup "salt water" and the other cup "water." Make sure to write on the tape.

Pour one-half cup of water into each paper cup. Add four teaspoons of salt to the cup marked "salt water." Stir the salt water until all the salt dissolves.

Place both cups into the freezer section of a refrigerator. One cup contains pure water. The other cup contains salt water. Leave both cups in the freezer overnight.

Observations

Remove both cups from the freezer. What do you see? Is the water frozen solid? Is the salt water still a liquid?

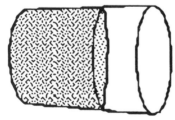

SOLID WATER

LIQUID
SALT WATER

Discussion

Water freezes at a temperature of 32 degrees Fahrenheit (0 degrees Celsius). When the temperature is below 32 degrees, then water molecules stick together and the liquid is changed into a solid. When the temperature is above 32 degrees, water molecules move faster and the solid is changed into a liquid. A refrigerator freezer is always colder than 32 degrees. The water froze because its temperature was below 32 degrees.

Salt water freezes at a lower temperature than water. The salt water does not freeze because the temperature is not low enough to make the salt water change to a solid. Table salt is <u>sodium chloride</u>. When sodium chloride is placed in water, it breaks into positive sodium ions and negative chlorine ions. The sodium and chlorine ions prevent the water molecules from getting next to each other and forming a solid.

It is often important to lower the temperature at which a liquid freezes. Think about the following three examples: A chemical called <u>ethylene glycol</u> (antifreeze) is added to the water in car radiators so the water will not freeze in the winter. Salt is sprinkled on icy pavements to melt ice. Salt is added to ice and water to make a mixture that is colder than 32 degrees. This cold salt water is used to freeze homemade ice cream.

Other things to try

Fill several cups with water. Add different amounts of salt to each cup. Find the least amount of salt you can add to keep the water from changing to a solid in your freezer.

Try this same experiment with sugar instead of salt.

22 ARE SOAP BUBBLES ATTRACTED BY A NEGATIVE CHARGE?

Materials

Soap bubble liquid and ring

A balloon

You can buy a bottle of soap bubble mix in toy stores and in many grocery stores, or you can mix dishwashing liquid with water to make your own soap bubble mix. Soap bubble kits come with a ring to blow bubbles. You can make your own ring from a piece of wire. Bend the wire to make a small loop.

Procedure

Blow up a balloon and tie it closed. Press the balloon against your hair or sweater. Rub the balloon back and forth over your hair or sweater about thirty times. Move the balloon rapidly back and forth as you keep it pressed against your hair or sweater.

With one hand hold the balloon out in front of you. Dip your soap bubble ring into the soapy liquid. Hold the ring in front of your mouth and blow soap bubbles into the air. Move the balloon toward the soap bubbles floating in the air.

Observations

What happens to the soap bubbles that come close to the balloon? Do they suddenly move toward the balloon? What happens when the soap bubbles touch the balloon?

Discussion

When the soap bubbles get near the balloon, they jump toward the balloon. The soap bubbles are pulled toward the balloon. The polar molecules in the bubbles are attracted to the negatively charged balloon.

Soap bubbles are made of soap molecules and water molecules. A soap molecule has a polar end and a nonpolar end. Water is a polar molecule. The polar ends of soap molecules are attracted to polar water molecules. The nonpolar ends of soap molecules are attracted to each other. The nonpolar ends of the soap molecules stick out from the water and help hold bubbles together.

As you rub the balloon against your hair or sweater, you rub electrons onto the balloon. Electrons are tiny particles that are found in all atoms. Atoms are made of positive protons, neutral neutrons, and negative electrons. The protons and neutrons stay in the center of an atom while electrons move around them. Electrons can sometimes be moved from one atom or molecule to another. Electrons that are rubbed onto the balloon give the balloon a negative charge. The negative balloon pulls on the positive part of the polar molecules in the bubbles. The

SOAP BUBBLES

CHARGED BALLOON

57

attraction between positive and negative charges is called <u>electrostatic</u> <u>attraction</u>.

Other things to try

Rub a balloon against your hair or sweater. Place the balloon on the wall. The balloon should stick to the wall because the balloon has a negative charge and is pulled toward the wall. After a while the balloon will fall because the extra electrons gradually go into the wall and the air. The balloon can be recharged with electrons by rubbing it in your hair or sweater again. Try rubbing the balloon on other types of material. Does the balloon pick up electrons from other things?

You can also use a plastic comb or plastic pen to attract soap bubbles. Run the comb through your hair or over a sweater about thirty times. Then blow bubbles and see if they are pulled toward the comb.

CAN ACIDS AND BASES BE IDENTIFIED WITH VEGETABLE MOLECULES?

Materials

Red cabbage leaves	Vinegar	A teaspoon
A large bowl	Baking soda	Tape
Three paper cups	Lemon juice	A felt pen
Hot water	A measuring cup	

Procedure

Put a piece of tape on each cup. Using the felt pen write "vinegar," "baking soda,"and "lemon juice" on the pieces of tape.

Tear several cabbage leaves into pieces about the size of your thumb. Put one cup of the cabbage pieces into a bowl. Use hot water from the sink faucet to fill a measuring cup. Add four cups of hot water to the bowl. Let the leaves sit in the water until the water turns dark purple. This should take about fifteen minutes. When the water is no longer hot, squeeze the leaves with your fingers to remove more of the color.

Pour one-half cup of the colored juice into the cup labeled "vinegar." Add one teaspoon of vinegar to this cup. Into the paper cup labeled "baking soda" pour one-half cup of the colored juice and add one teaspoon of baking soda. Into the cup labeled "lemon juice" pour one-half cup of the colored juice and add several drops of lemon juice.

Observations

What color does the cabbage juice turn when you add the vinegar? What color does the cabbage juice turn when you add the baking soda? What color does the cabbage juice turn when you add lemon juice?

Discussion

Some molecules, like those in the red cabbage juice, can be used to identify other molecules as <u>acids</u> or <u>bases</u>. These identifying molecules are called <u>indicators</u> because they will change color. They have a different color in an acid and a different color in a base.

LEMON JUICE   **BAKING SODA**

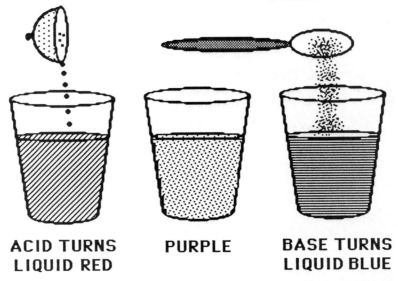

ACID TURNS   **PURPLE**   **BASE TURNS**
LIQUID RED   **LIQUID BLUE**

Acids and bases are common chemicals used every day. Some acids and bases are harmful if touched or swallowed. Some acids and bases are found in foods and are not harmful. Many acids and bases can be found around the home. Common household acids include acetic acid in vinegar, citric acid in lemon juice, and lactic acid in sour milk. It is the acids in these foods which give them their sour taste. Bases are the chemical opposites of acids. Baking soda is a base.

Acids and bases neutralize each other when they are mixed. When acids are added to the cabbage juice, some of the molecules in the cabbage juice change their color to red. When bases are added to the cabbage juice, some of the molecules in the cabbage juice change color to blue. Do you see how the purple cabbage juice can be used to identify acids and bases?

Other Things to Try

Try other foods from your home to see if they contain molecules that are acids or bases. Are Rolaids an acid or a base (Rolaids are a registered trademark of the Warner-Lambert Company)? Is 7-Up an acid or a base (7-Up is a registered trademark of the 7-Up Company)?

Other colored vegetables can be used to make indicators. Try to make an indicator from grape juice, cherries, onions, beets, apple skins, or tea.

In a large bowl in the kitchen sink, add the red colored cabbage juice containing the vinegar to the blue colored cabbage juice containing the baking soda. Fizzing will occur. What color is the liquid when the fizzing stops? If it is purple this shows that acids and bases are chemical opposites and they neutralize each other. When they neutralize each other the original color of the cabbage juice returns.

24 DOES ACID RAIN HURT SOME BUILDINGS AND STATUES?

Materials

Two pieces of chalk, each one inch long	Water
Two small bowls	Tape
Vinegar	A felt pen

Procedure

Put a piece of tape on each bowl. Using a felt pen write "water" on one piece of tape and "vinegar" on the other piece of tape.

Place a piece of chalk in each bowl. Fill one bowl with water. Fill the other bowl with vinegar.

Observations

Watch the bowls for several minutes. Do you see bubbles of gas in the bowl with the vinegar? Where do these bubbles form? Are there bubbles in the bowl of water?

Leave the chalk in the bowls overnight. Are there still bubbles of gas in the bowl with the vinegar? Now take the pieces of chalk out of the water and out of the vinegar. Is the chalk that was left in the vinegar overnight smaller than the chalk that was in the water?

Discussion

There are many different types of acids. Lemon juice and vinegar are common acids. Vinegar is a mixture of acetic acid and water.

In some parts of the world, there is more acid in the rain than normal. This type of rain is called <u>acid rain</u>. Scientists believe that one cause of acid rain is sulfur dioxide. <u>Sulfur dioxide</u> is a type of air pollution produced by burning fuels that contain sulfur atoms. When

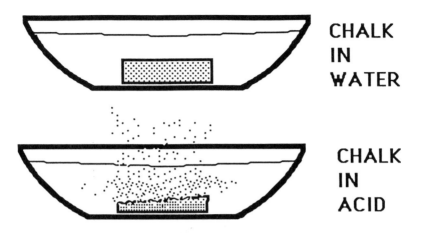

CHALK IN WATER

CHALK IN ACID

sulfur dioxide gets in rain water, it produces <u>sulfuric acid</u>. Sulfuric acid is one cause of acid rain. Acid rain can harm fish and trees, and even buildings. Scientists are working to understand acid rain and to control it.

Chalk is made of a mineral called <u>limestone</u>. Another name for limestone is <u>calcium carbonate</u>. Limestone is sometimes used to make buildings. Limestone has been used for many years to make statues. Some Greek statues thousands of years old are made of limestone.

When acid gets on limestone, the calcium carbonate is broken apart. Calcium ions and carbon dioxide gas are two of the things that are formed. The bubbles you see in the bowl with the vinegar are carbon dioxide. The bubbles form on the surface of the chalk. The chalk in the vinegar gets smaller because the acetic acid in the vinegar breaks the calcium carbonate in the chalk apart. Acid rain can hurt statues and buildings in the same way.

Other things to try

Cover a piece of chalk with lemon or grapefruit juice. Watch the bubbles of carbon dioxide that are made. Pour out the juice and pour water over the chalk. Do the bubbles stop? The bubbles will stop if there is no acid on the chalk.

25 CAN IONS CARRY ELECTRICITY?

Materials

A 6-volt lantern battery   Two paper clips

A 6-volt flashlight bulb   A jar of water

Two pieces of insulated wire (each about twelve inches long)

Salt

Procedure

ASK AN ADULT TO HELP YOU WITH THIS EXPERIMENT. ELECTRICITY CAN BE DANGEROUS. NEVER PUT HOUSE CURRENT (electricity from a wall outlet) IN WATER. YOU SHOULD ONLY USE A SMALL BATTERY FOR THIS EXPERIMENT. DO NOT LET ANY FLAME GET NEAR YOUR EXPERIMENT.

Ask an adult to remove about one-half inch of insulation from each end of the two wires. Connect one paper clip to the negative (-) terminal on the battery. Bend the paper clip so it sticks down into the water. Connect a wire to the other paper clip. Place the other paper clip over the edge of the jar and into the water. You need to have at least an inch of each paper clip under the water. Connect the other wire to the positive (+) terminal on the battery.

Wrap the end of one wire around the light bulb as illustrated. Grasp the insulated part of the other wire and hold the end of the wire against the bottom of the bulb to complete the circuit. Now begin to sprinkle salt into the jar of water. Continue sprinkling the salt until the light bulb begins to glow. DO NOT LET THE ELEC-TRICITY FLOW THROUGH THE WATER FOR MORE THAN A FEW MINUTES SO THAT ONLY A SMALL AMOUNT OF HYDROGEN GAS IS PRODUCED.

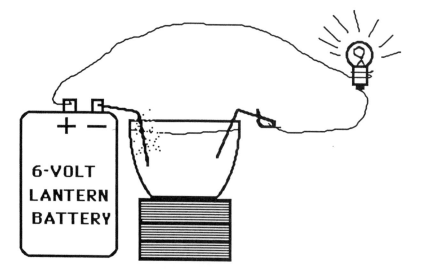

ELECTRICITY GOES THROUGH SALT WATER

If the bulb does not come on then you have a loose wire, bad connection, or a dead battery. Check all the wires.

Observations

When you first start to sprinkle salt in the water is the bulb off? After you sprinkle salt in the water, does the bulb begin to glow? What makes the bulb come on?

Discussion

The battery produces electrons at the negative (-) terminal when the circuit is complete. These electrons flow through the wire and through the light bulb. The electrons return to the battery at the positive (+) terminal. Electrons moving in a wire are called electricity. These moving electrons cause the bulb to give off light.

Charged atoms or groups of atoms are called <u>ions</u>. Ions help carry electricity through the water. Positive ions in the water pick up electrons at the negative paper clip. Negative ions in the water give up electrons at the positive paper clip. Opposite charges attract.

Salt is made of sodium and chlorine ions. The sodium ions have a positive charge. The chlorine ions have a negative charge. When you add salt to water, you are adding positive and negative ions to the water. There are other ions in water, but not enough to carry the electricity through the water to light the bulb. The flashlight bulb does not come on until you add salt to the water.

You see small bubbles at the negative paper clip. These bubbles are hydrogen gas. Hydrogen gas will burn. YOU SHOULD NOT GET A FLAME NEAR THE HYDROGEN GAS. The hydrogen gas comes from hydrogen ions found in water. When two positive hydrogen ions pick up electrons, they combine to form a hydrogen gas molecule. Each hydrogen gas molecule is made of two hydrogen atoms.

Other things to try

Repeat this experiment, but add sugar instead of salt to the water. Sugar should not make the bulb light because sugar molecules are not made of ions. Sugar molecules cannot carry electricity.

WILL METAL ATOMS COMBINE WITH OXYGEN MOLECULES? 26

Materials

Two new, shiny pennies

One old, brown penny

Aluminum foil

A metal cookie sheet

An oven

A pot holder

Procedure

ASK AN ADULT TO HELP YOU WITH THIS EXPERIMENT. DO NOT USE THE OVEN BY YOURSELF. Put a piece of aluminum foil on a metal cookie sheet. Put one shiny, new penny on the aluminum foil. Put the cookie sheet in the oven. Close the oven. Turn the oven to 400 degrees. Wait at least thirty minutes. Turn the oven off. Use a pot holder to remove the cookie sheet. Place the cookie sheet on top the stove. Do not touch the penny until it has cooled.

Observations

What color is the new penny that you heated? Compare it to the other new penny and the old, brown penny. Does it look like a new penny or an old penny?

Discussion

Since 1982 pennies are made of zinc metal coated with copper metal. Older pennies are made of only copper. The copper atoms on the surface of the penny can combine with oxygen gas in the air. The copper atoms and oxygen molecules combine to form copper oxide. Copper metal is shiny and bright. Copper oxide is brown or black and is not shiny.

The penny you heat in the oven no longer looks like a new penny. It is not shiny and bright because now it is covered with copper oxide. It looks like an old penny.

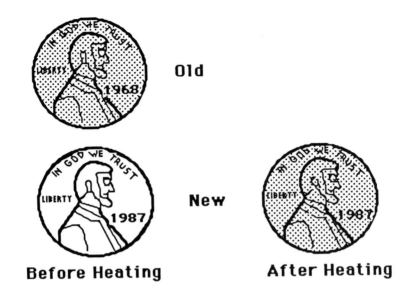

Old

New

Before Heating   After Heating

It may take several years for a brown copper oxide layer to form on the surface of a penny. You make this change go faster by heating a new penny in an oven. If you had not heated the penny, you would have to wait more than a year before it would turn brown. The high temperature in the oven makes the molecules combine faster.

Other things to try

Look at a bunch of pennies. Compare the dates on the pennies with their color. Are the old pennies usually brown? Are the new pennies usually shiny and bright? Can you explain why they are different?

Pennies that are the same age are not always the same color. Pennies that have been touched more often will turn darker more quickly. The moisture on your hands gets on pennies and the water speeds up the combination of oxygen molecules and copper atoms. Coin collectors sometimes cover shiny new coins with plastic to keep air and water from touching the coins.

Repeat this experiment using other new coins such as a nickel, a dime, and a quarter.

CAN LIGHT BE MADE BY BREAKING SUGAR CRYSTALS?   **27**

Materials

Wint-o-green Lifesavers

(Lifesavers are a registered trademark of Lifesaver, Inc.)

A clear plastic sandwich bag

Pliers

Procedure

Use Wint-o-green Lifesavers that contain sugar. This experiment does not work with sugar-free Wint-o-green Lifesavers. Place the Lifesaver in a clear plastic sandwich bag. Tie the bag with a garbage twist. Hold the wrapped Lifesaver in the jaws of the pliers. Turn out the lights. Make sure the room is totally dark. Wait about one minute to allow your eyes to adjust to the darkness. While looking very closely at the Lifesaver squeeze the pliers to crush the Lifesaver inside the bag. You must look carefully when crushing the Lifesaver to see the light.

Having the Lifesaver in the bag makes the experiment safer and easier to clean up.

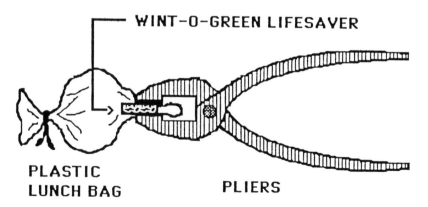

WINT-O-GREEN LIFESAVER

PLASTIC
LUNCH BAG

PLIERS

Observations

What color is the Wint-o-green Lifesaver? Do you see a flash of light when the Lifesaver is crushed? What color is the light? How long does the light last? Does the Lifesaver crumble into many pieces?

Discussion

Light can be made by chemical processes, by electricity, or by mechanical stress. Fireflies make light by chemical processes. Electricity is used to make light in light bulbs. In this experiment mechanical stress is used to make light. Grinding and crushing are mechanical stresses.

Wint-o-green Lifesavers are made of sucrose crystals. Sucrose is the chemical name for table sugar. Wint-o-green Lifesavers also contain flavor molecules that give them a wintergreen taste. When pliers are used to crush a Lifesaver, sugar crystals are broken. This causes gas molecules inside the crystals to obtain extra energy.

Molecules that obtain extra energy are called excited molecules. The extra energy in the excited gas molecules is quickly given off as light. Light is a form of energy. The flavor molecules in the Lifesaver also become excited molecules when the sucrose molecules are broken. The flavor molecules also give off light. A soft blue-white light is made when a Wint-o-green Lifesaver is crushed.

Other things to try

Place a sugar-free Wint-o-green Lifesaver in a plastic bag and crush it with the pliers. You should not see any light because there are no sugar molecules in the Lifesaver.

70

Can you see light when you crush with pliers a wintergreen flavored Certs mint in a plastic bag (Certs is a registered trademark of Warner-Lambert Co.)?

Try other hard candies to see if they give off light when they are crushed with pliers in a plastic bag.

28 CAN ETHYLENE MOLECULES CAUSE FRUITS AND VEGETABLES TO RIPEN?

Materials

An overripe banana

Two green tomatoes

A shoe box with a lid

Procedure

Place the overripe banana in the shoe box. An overripe banana has dark spots on its skin and is soft. Place one of the green tomatoes in the shoe box with the very ripe banana. Place the lid on the shoe box. Set the other green tomato close by, but outside the shoebox. It may take several days to see any changes. Open the box only once a day to take a quick look at the tomato. If the box is left open too long the experiment will not work because the ethylene gas will escape from the box.

SHOE BOX

OVERRIPE BANANA   GREEN TOMATO

Observations

Are the green tomatoes soft or firm? Does the tomato in the shoe box turn red faster than the one outside the shoe box? How long does it take

72

for the tomato in the shoe box to turn red? How long does it take for the tomato outside the shoe box to turn red? Is the tomato that ripened in the shoe box soft or firm?

Discussion

Hormones are chemicals made by plants and animals. Hormones control living processes. The ripening of fruit is a process controlled by hormones. Ethylene gas is a hormone made by fruits while they are ripening.

In this experiment an overripe banana is used to make ethylene gas molecules. To catch the ethylene gas, the overripe banana is kept in a closed shoe box. When the green tomato is placed in the shoe box, the ethylene molecules from the overripe banana cause the green fruit to ripen rapidly. The tomato in the shoe box turns red faster than the tomato outside of the shoe box. Sometimes tomatoes and other fruits are taken from farms to cities and then treated with ethylene gas to ripen them. This process is called artificial ripening.

Other things to try

Try ripening other fruits and vegetables with ethylene molecules. Try green strawberries, green peaches or green bananas.

Try using overripe avocados to ripen green tomatoes. Overripe avocados produce a lot of ethylene molecules.

Have you ever heard the saying, "One bad apple spoils the whole barrel?" A bad apple is one that is rotten. It produces a lot of ethylene gas. The ethylene gas then causes the other apples to turn bad.

29 CAN CERTAIN MOLECULES IN THE AIR CAUSE FOOD TO SPOIL?

Materials

An apple	Lemon juice
A knife	A plate
A bowl of cold water	

Procedure

ASK AN ADULT TO HELP YOU CUT AN APPLE INTO FOUR PIECES. Immediately place two pieces of apple in a bowl of cold water. Rub the third piece of apple with lemon juice. Place this piece of apple on the plate. Place the fourth piece of apple on the plate. Observe the pieces of apple every ten minutes for at least one-half hour or longer.

Observations

What color are the apple pieces when they are first sliced? How long does it take for the apple slices to turn brown? Which apple slice turns brown first? Do all of the apple slices turn brown?

Discussion

Certain fruits and vegetables turn brown when they are sliced. Fresh apples and bananas turn brown when they are sliced. Fruit turns brown because of a chemical reaction. In this <u>chemical reaction</u> some molecules are changed into different molecules. In this experiment we are studying the chemical reaction that causes apples to turn brown.

When an apple is sliced, the inside part of the apple is surrounded by air. Air contains oxygen molecules. Oxygen molecules in the air combine with molecules in the apple to turn the apple brown.

Large, complex molecules in the fruit cause the combination of oxygen molecules and certain molecules in the apple to occur faster.

COLD WATER	LEMON JUICE	NOTHING

These large, complex molecules are called <u>enzymes</u>. The piece of apple that is left in the air turns brown because of these enzyme molecules.

The two pieces of apple that are in the bowl of cold water do not turn brown because each piece is surrounded by water molecules. The water molecules keep oxygen molecules from adding to molecules in the apple.

The piece of apple that is rubbed with lemon juice does not turn brown because molecules in the lemon juice change the enzymes in the apple. When the enzymes are changed, they cannot cause the oxygen molecules to add to molecules in the apple. Lemon or citrus juice may be added to fresh fruit in a fruit salad to keep the fruit from turning brown.

Other things to try

Remove one of the pieces of apple that is in the bowl of cold water. Does it turn brown after sitting in the air for thirty minutes?

ASK AN ADULT TO HELP YOU CUT AN APPLE INTO PIECES. Put a piece of apple in a bowl of hot water. Remove the piece of apple after five minutes. Does this piece of apple turn brown when exposed to air? Even though this piece of apple is now exposed to oxygen molecules it should not turn brown since the heat changes the enzyme molecules.

Do fresh peaches turn brown when they are sliced? See if lemon juice will stop sliced fresh peaches and bananas from turning brown.

30 CAN SUGAR BE CHANGED TO CARBON?

Materials

Aluminum foil	An oven
A teaspoon	A metal cookie sheet
Sugar	A pot holder

Procedure

ASK AN ADULT TO HELP YOU. DO NOT USE THE OVEN BY YOURSELF.

Put a piece of aluminum foil on a metal cookie sheet. Place a fourth of a teaspoon of sugar on the aluminum foil. Put the tray in the oven. Turn the oven to 400 degrees Fahrenheit. Wait fifteen minutes. Turn the oven off. Use a pot holder to remove the cookie sheet from the oven and place the cookie sheet on the stove. Do not touch the cookie sheet until it has cooled.

Observations

What color is sugar? What color is the sugar after it is heated in the oven? Does the heated sugar look different? Does the heated sugar feel different? Does heating the sugar cause a smell to fill the air?

Discussion

Sugar is a white solid in the form of small grains. Each grain is made of many sugar molecules. When sugar is heated to a high temperature it is changed to carbon. Carbon is a black solid. The small, white grains of sugar have been changed to a black lump of carbon.

There are many different types of sugar molecules. The type of sugar you use at home is called <u>sucrose</u> (cane sugar). Each sucrose molecule is made of atoms of carbon, hydrogen, and oxygen. When sugar molecules are heated to very high temperatures, each molecule breaks apart. Water molecules are formed and are given off as a gas. Each water molecule is made of two hydrogen atoms and one oxygen atom. As water molecules are released, carbon atoms are left behind. Other gases are also given off (you may be able to smell them in the kitchen), and there may be a complex mixture of molecules left behind.

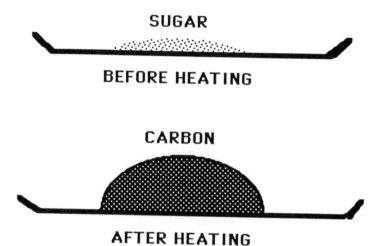

SUGAR

BEFORE HEATING

CARBON

AFTER HEATING

If you pick up the piece of carbon, you can feel that it is very light. If you look at the bottom of the carbon, you will see small holes in the solid. These holes are made from gases that are produced during heating.

Other things to try

Marshmallows contain sugar. Can you explain why a white marshmallow turns black if it gets too hot? Have you ever seen someone burn toast by leaving it in a toaster too long?

COMPLETE LIST OF MATERIALS
USED IN THESE EXPERIMENTS

almond extract
aluminum foil
apple
apple cider vinegar
avocado

baking soda
balloon
bananas
beets
bottle opener
bowl

Certs
chalk
cherries
chili powder
cinnamon
clear plastic sandwich bags
coins
Coke
cooking oil
corn syrup

dishwashing liquid
distilled white vinegar
drinking glasses

Epsom salt

felt pen
flour
food coloring

golf balls
grape juice
grapefruit juice
grocery bags
gumdrops

hard candies

ice cubes
insulated wire
Ivory Soap

jars with lids

kitchen sink
knife

lemon extract
lemon juice
lime juice

marshmallows
measuring cups
metal cookie sheet
meter stick

onions
oregano leaves
oven

pan
paper clips
paper cups
paper towels
parsley
peaches
pennies
pepper
plastic ballpoint pen
plastic comb
plastic pail
plate
pliers
pot holders

racquetballs
red cabbage leaves
refrigerator freezer
Rolaids
rubber balls
rubber band

salt
sand

scissors
7-Up
shoe box with a lid
6-volt flashlight bulb
6-volt lantern battery
soap bubble liquid and ring
soft drink bottle
spoon
strawberries
string
sugar

tablespoon
tape
tea
teaspoon
tennis balls
tomatoes
toothpicks

vanilla extract

water
wax paper
Wint-o-green Lifesavers
wire

yardstick
yeast

INDEX